I0048626

TABLE OF CONTENTS

TABLE OF CONTENTS

#	SUBJECT	PAGE

TABLE OF CONTENTS

#	SUBJECT	PAGE

YEARLY INCOME & EXPENSES

YEAR : ....

MONTH	INCOME	EXPENSES	BALANCE	NOTES
TOTAL				

NOTES

_____
_____
_____
_____
_____
_____
_____
_____
_____
_____
_____
_____
_____
_____

YEARLY INCOME & EXPENSES

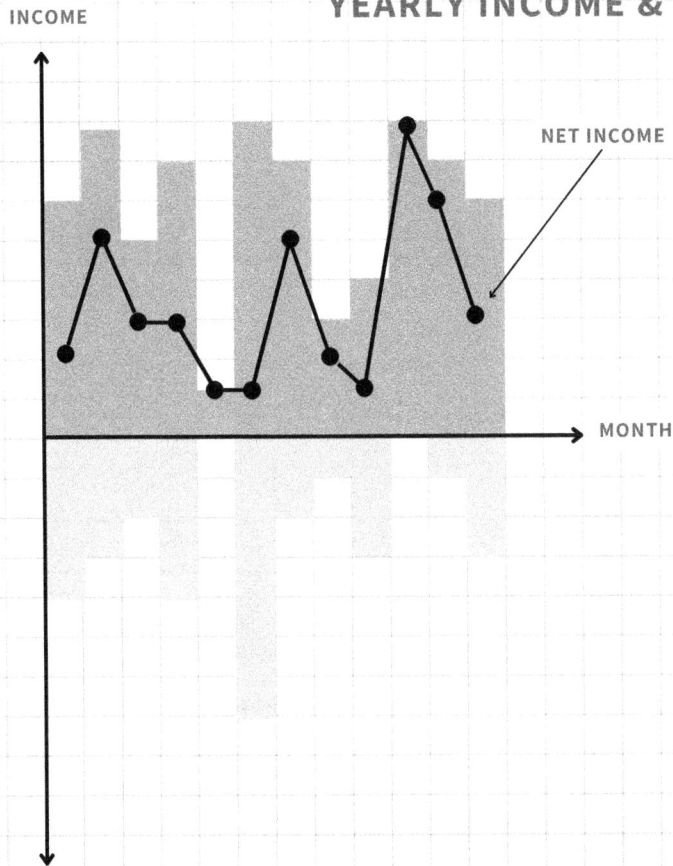

INCOME

MONTH

NET INCOME

EXPENSES

HOW TO:

BUILD YOUR CHART USING YOUR MONTHLY INCOME & EXPENSES SUMMARIES:

- CALCULATE YOUR SCALE USING THE HIGHEST NUMBER IN TERMS OF INCOME OR EXPENSES PER MONTH AND DIVIDE IT BY 10 TO GET THE SIZE OF A SQUARE ON THE Y AXIS
- PLOT YOUR TOTAL MONTHLY INCOME AS POSITIVE BARS ON THE Y-AXIS AND YOUR TOTAL MONTHLY EXPENSES AS NEGATIVE BARS ON THE Y-AXIS (DIVIDE MONTHLY INCOME/EXPENSE BY THE SIZE OF A SQUARE TO FIND THE NUMBER OF SQUARES TO FILL)
- BUILD YOUR NET INCOME LINE CHART USING YOUR MONTHLY BALANCE

YEAR:

NOTES:

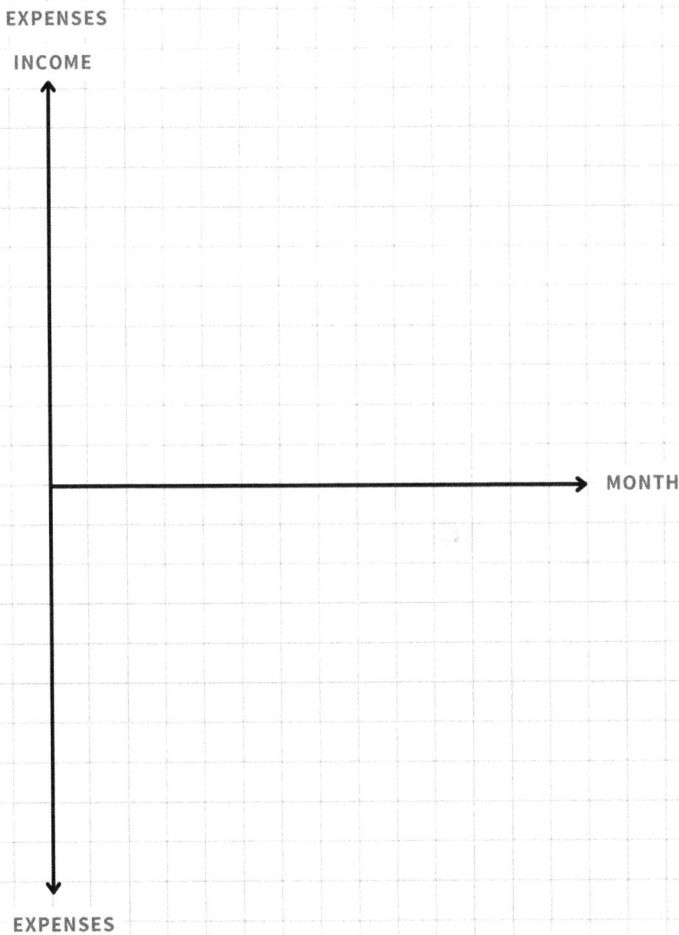

INCOME

MONTH

EXPENSES

MONTHLY INCOME & EXPENSES SUMMARY

MONTH : ....

DATE	DAY	INCOME	EXPENSES	BALANCE	NOTES
1					
2					
3					
4					
5					
6					
7					
8					
9					
10					
11					
12					
13					
14					
15					
16					
17					
18					
19					
20					
21					
22					
23					
24					
25					
26					
27					
28					
29					
30					
31					
TOTAL					

MONTHLY INCOME & EXPENSES CHART

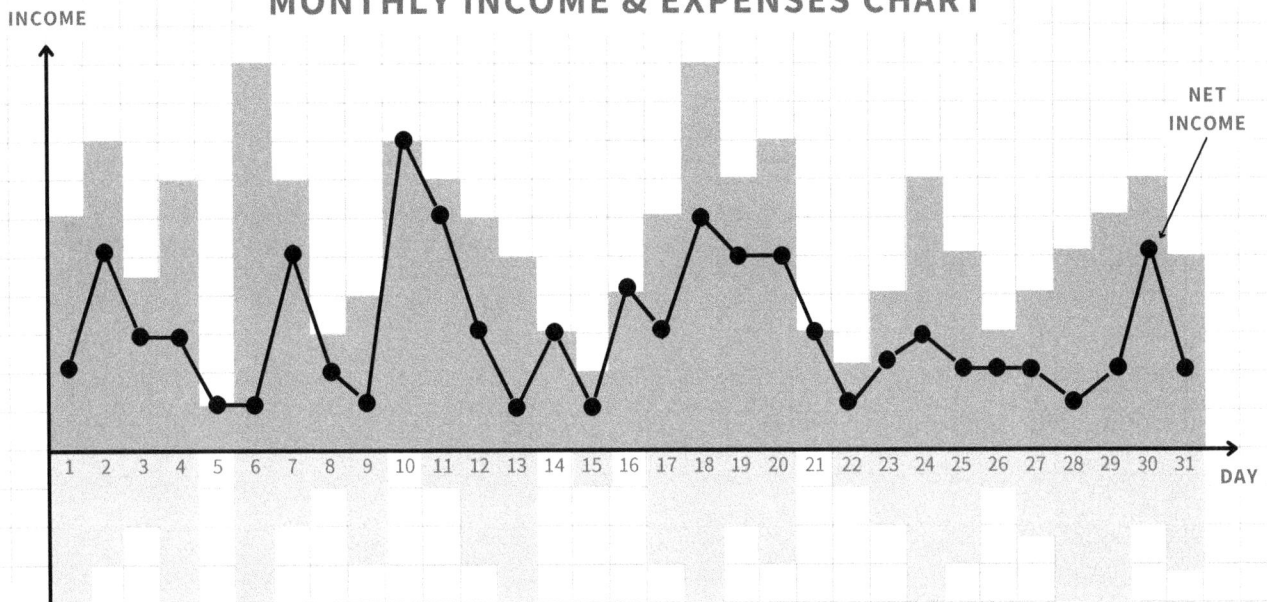

INCOME

NET INCOME

1 2 3 4 5 6 7 8 9 10 11 12 13 14 15 16 17 18 19 20 21 22 23 24 25 26 27 28 29 30 31 DAY

EXPENSES

HOW TO:

BUILD YOUR CHART USING YOUR MONTHLY INCOME & EXPENSES SUMMARY:
- CALCULATE YOUR SCALE USING THE HIGHEST NUMBER IN TERMS OF INCOME OR EXPENSES PER DAY AND DIVIDE IT BY 10 TO GET THE SIZE OF A SQUARE ON THE Y AXIS
- PLOT YOUR TOTAL DAILY INCOME AS POSITIVE BARS ON THE Y-AXIS AND YOUR TOTAL DAILY EXPENSES AS NEGATIVE BARS ON THE Y-AXIS (DIVIDE DAILY INCOME/EXPENSE BY THE SIZE OF A SQUARE TO FIND THE NUMBER OF SQUARES TO FILL)
- BUILD YOUR NET INCOME LINE CHART USING YOUR DAILY BALANCE

MONTH:

INCOME

DAY

EXPENSES

4

MONTHLY INCOME & EXPENSES SUMMARY

MONTH : ....

DATE	DAY	INCOME	EXPENSES	BALANCE	NOTES
1					
2					
3					
4					
5					
6					
7					
8					
9					
10					
11					
12					
13					
14					
15					
16					
17					
18					
19					
20					
21					
22					
23					
24					
25					
26					
27					
28					
29					
30					
31					
TOTAL					

MONTHLY INCOME & EXPENSES CHART

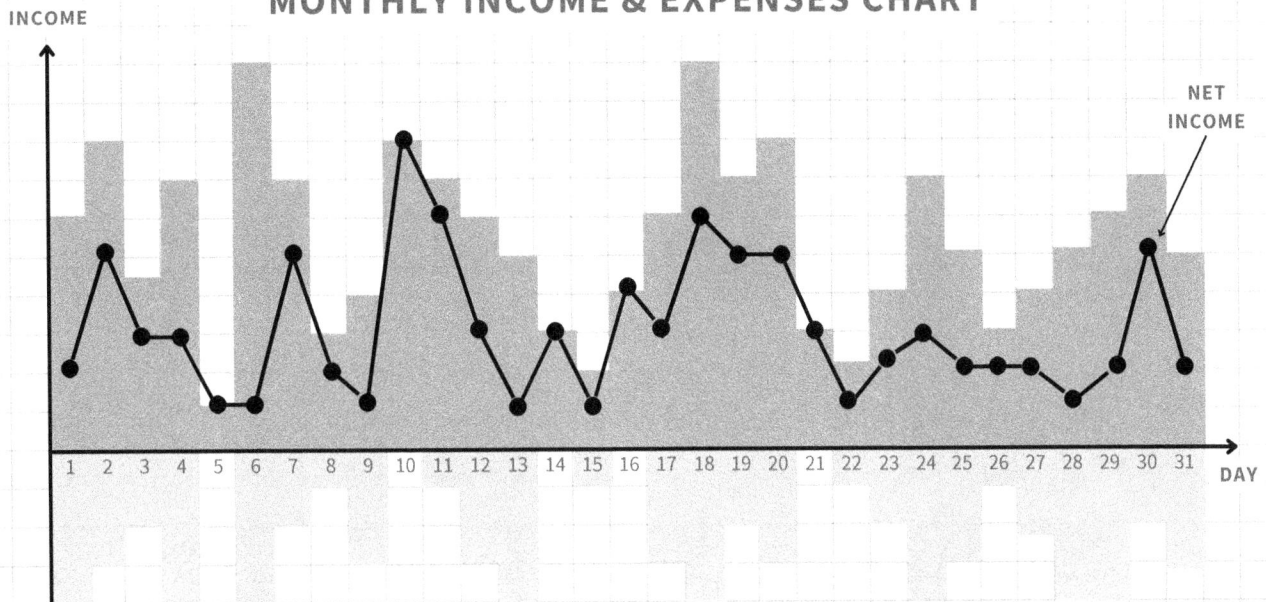

HOW TO:

BUILD YOUR CHART USING YOUR MONTHLY INCOME & EXPENSES SUMMARY:

- CALCULATE YOUR SCALE USING THE HIGHEST NUMBER IN TERMS OF INCOME OR EXPENSES PER DAY AND DIVIDE IT BY 10 TO GET THE SIZE OF A SQUARE ON THE Y AXIS
- PLOT YOUR TOTAL DAILY INCOME AS POSITIVE BARS ON THE Y-AXIS AND YOUR TOTAL DAILY EXPENSES AS NEGATIVE BARS ON THE Y-AXIS (DIVIDE DAILY INCOME/EXPENSE BY THE SIZE OF A SQUARE TO FIND THE NUMBER OF SQUARES TO FILL)
- BUILD YOUR NET INCOME LINE CHART USING YOUR DAILY BALANCE

MONTH:

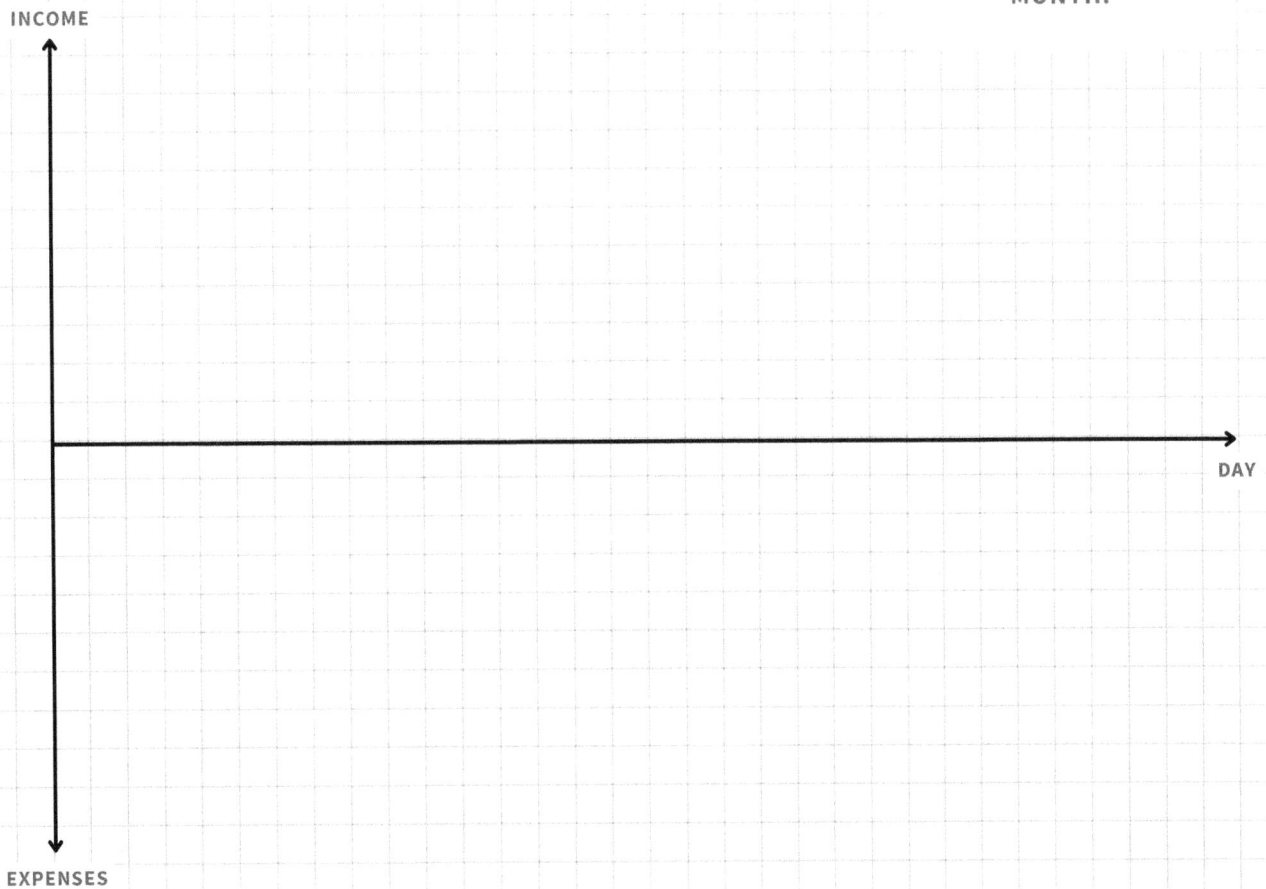

6

MONTHLY INCOME & EXPENSES SUMMARY

MONTH : ....

DATE	DAY	INCOME	EXPENSES	BALANCE	NOTES
1					
2					
3					
4					
5					
6					
7					
8					
9					
10					
11					
12					
13					
14					
15					
16					
17					
18					
19					
20					
21					
22					
23					
24					
25					
26					
27					
28					
29					
30					
31					
TOTAL					

MONTHLY INCOME & EXPENSES CHART

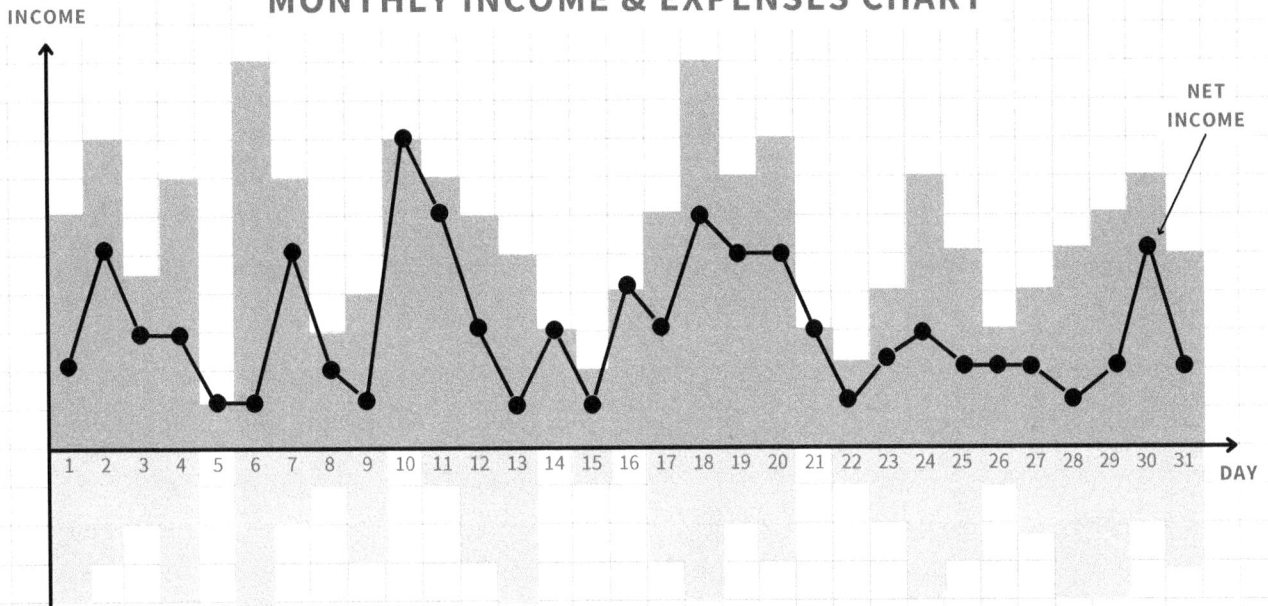

HOW TO:

BUILD YOUR CHART USING YOUR MONTHLY INCOME & EXPENSES SUMMARY:

- CALCULATE YOUR SCALE USING THE HIGHEST NUMBER IN TERMS OF INCOME OR EXPENSES PER DAY AND DIVIDE IT BY 10 TO GET THE SIZE OF A SQUARE ON THE Y AXIS
- PLOT YOUR TOTAL DAILY INCOME AS POSITIVE BARS ON THE Y-AXIS AND YOUR TOTAL DAILY EXPENSES AS NEGATIVE BARS ON THE Y-AXIS (DIVIDE DAILY INCOME/EXPENSE BY THE SIZE OF A SQUARE TO FIND THE NUMBER OF SQUARES TO FILL)
- BUILD YOUR NET INCOME LINE CHART USING YOUR DAILY BALANCE

MONTH:

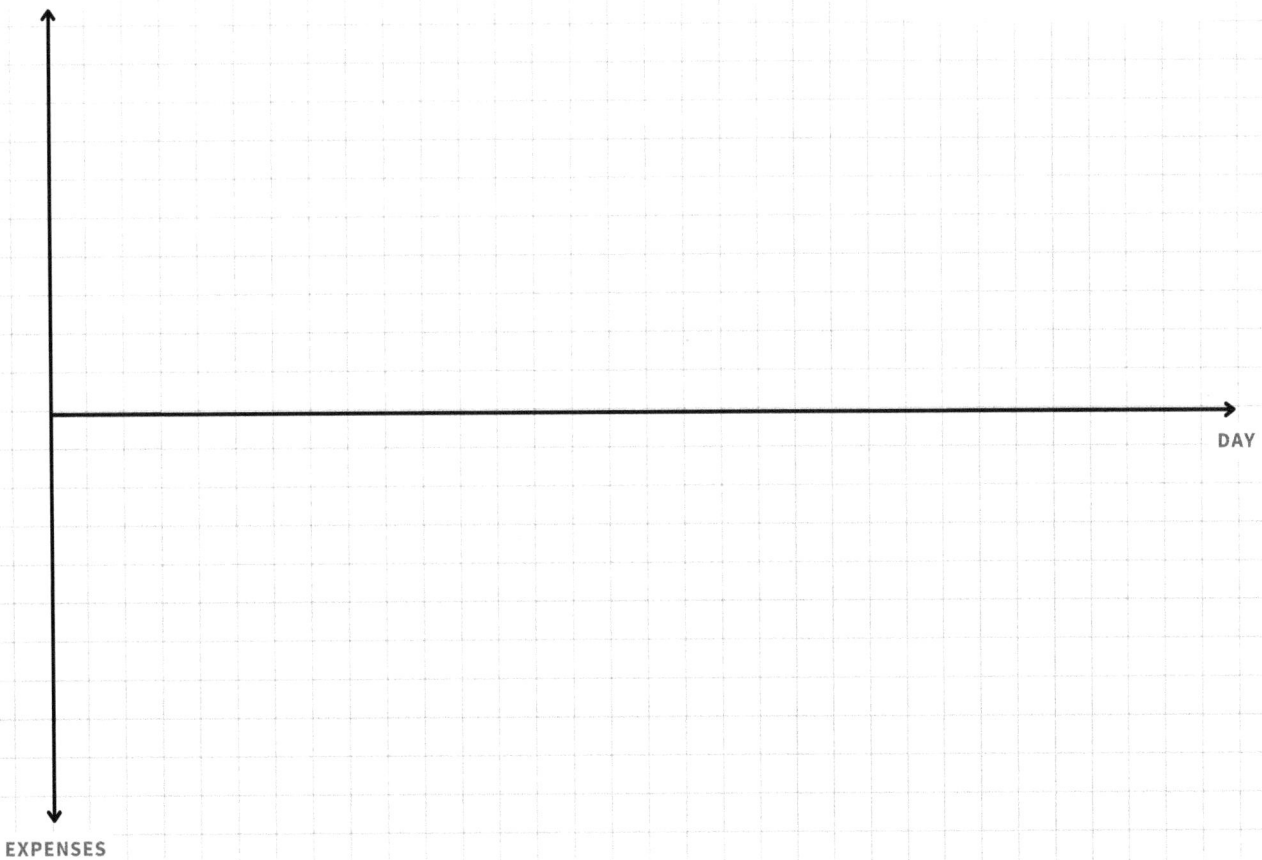

MONTHLY INCOME & EXPENSES SUMMARY

MONTH : ....

DATE	DAY	INCOME	EXPENSES	BALANCE	NOTES
1					
2					
3					
4					
5					
6					
7					
8					
9					
10					
11					
12					
13					
14					
15					
16					
17					
18					
19					
20					
21					
22					
23					
24					
25					
26					
27					
28					
29					
30					
31					
TOTAL					

MONTHLY INCOME & EXPENSES CHART

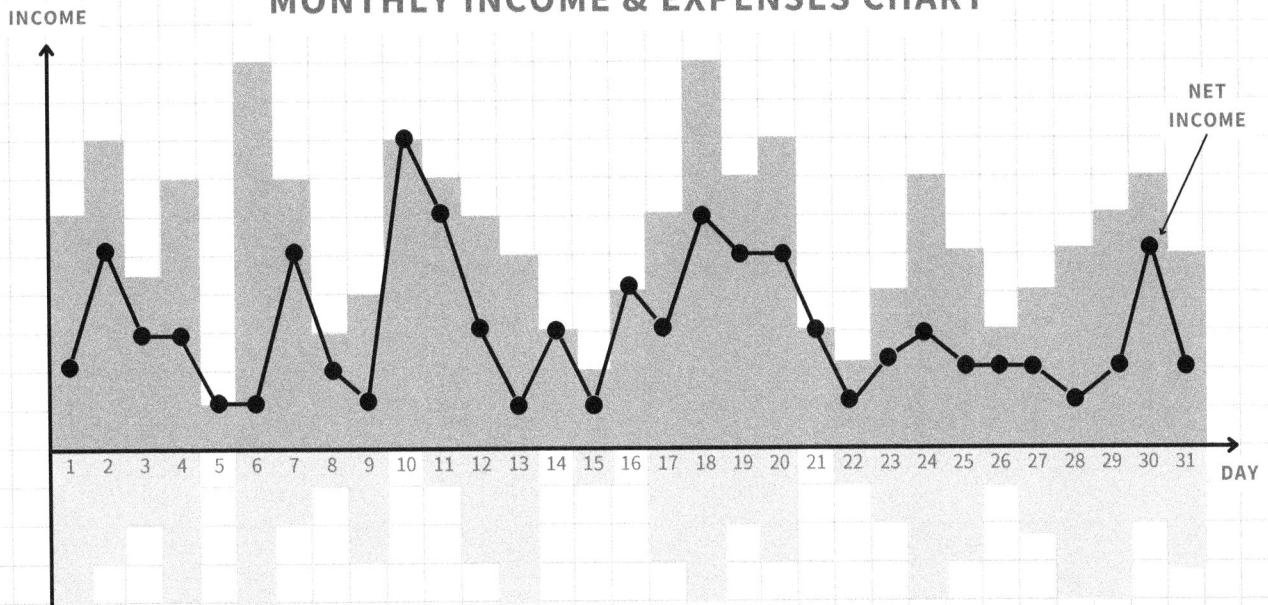

INCOME

NET INCOME

1 2 3 4 5 6 7 8 9 10 11 12 13 14 15 16 17 18 19 20 21 22 23 24 25 26 27 28 29 30 31 DAY

EXPENSES

HOW TO:
BUILD YOUR CHART USING YOUR MONTHLY INCOME & EXPENSES SUMMARY:
- CALCULATE YOUR SCALE USING THE HIGHEST NUMBER IN TERMS OF INCOME OR EXPENSES PER DAY AND DIVIDE IT BY 10 TO GET THE SIZE OF A SQUARE ON THE Y AXIS
- PLOT YOUR TOTAL DAILY INCOME AS POSITIVE BARS ON THE Y-AXIS AND YOUR TOTAL DAILY EXPENSES AS NEGATIVE BARS ON THE Y-AXIS (DIVIDE DAILY INCOME/EXPENSE BY THE SIZE OF A SQUARE TO FIND THE NUMBER OF SQUARES TO FILL)
- BUILD YOUR NET INCOME LINE CHART USING YOUR DAILY BALANCE

MONTH:

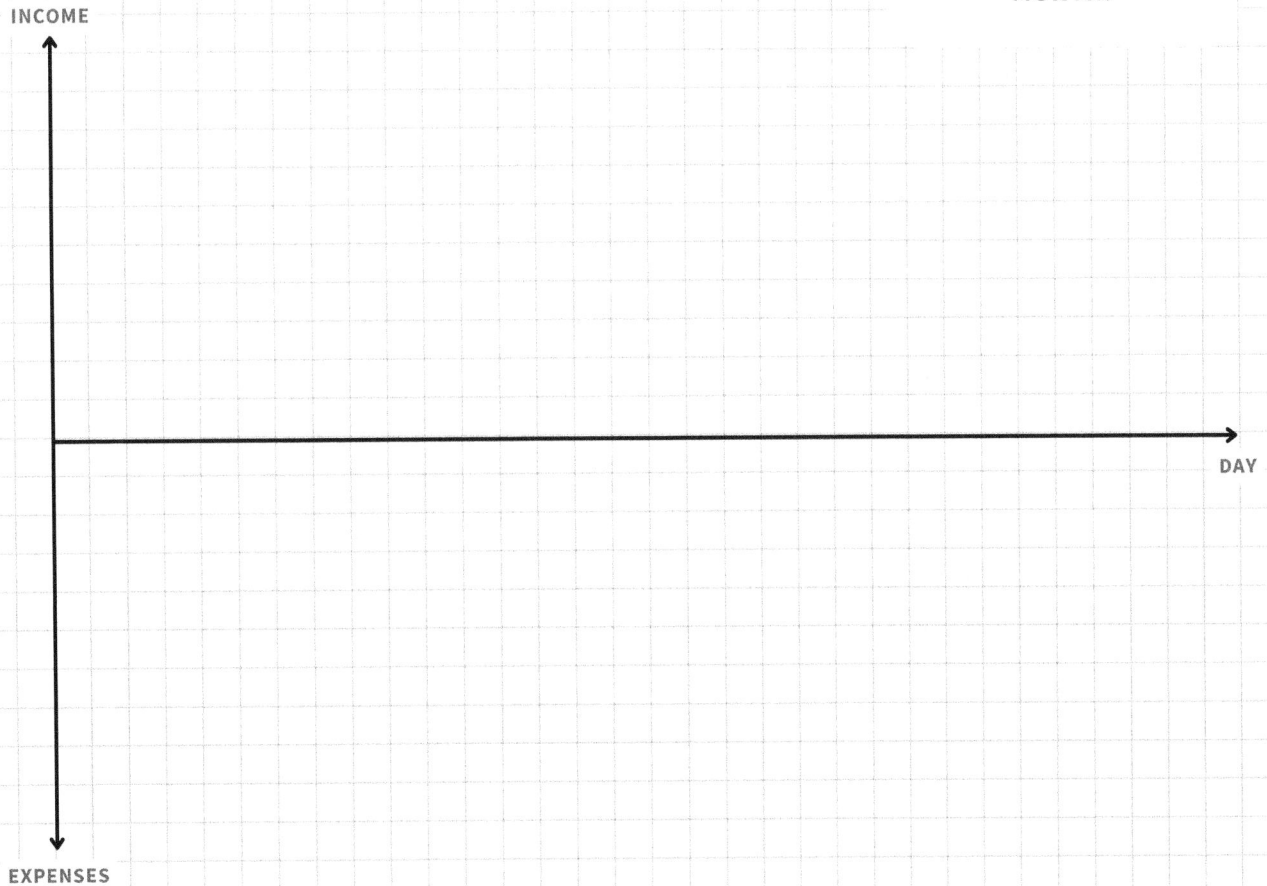

INCOME

DAY

EXPENSES

MONTHLY INCOME & EXPENSES SUMMARY

MONTH : ....

DATE	DAY	INCOME	EXPENSES	BALANCE	NOTES
1					
2					
3					
4					
5					
6					
7					
8					
9					
10					
11					
12					
13					
14					
15					
16					
17					
18					
19					
20					
21					
22					
23					
24					
25					
26					
27					
28					
29					
30					
31					
TOTAL					

MONTHLY INCOME & EXPENSES CHART

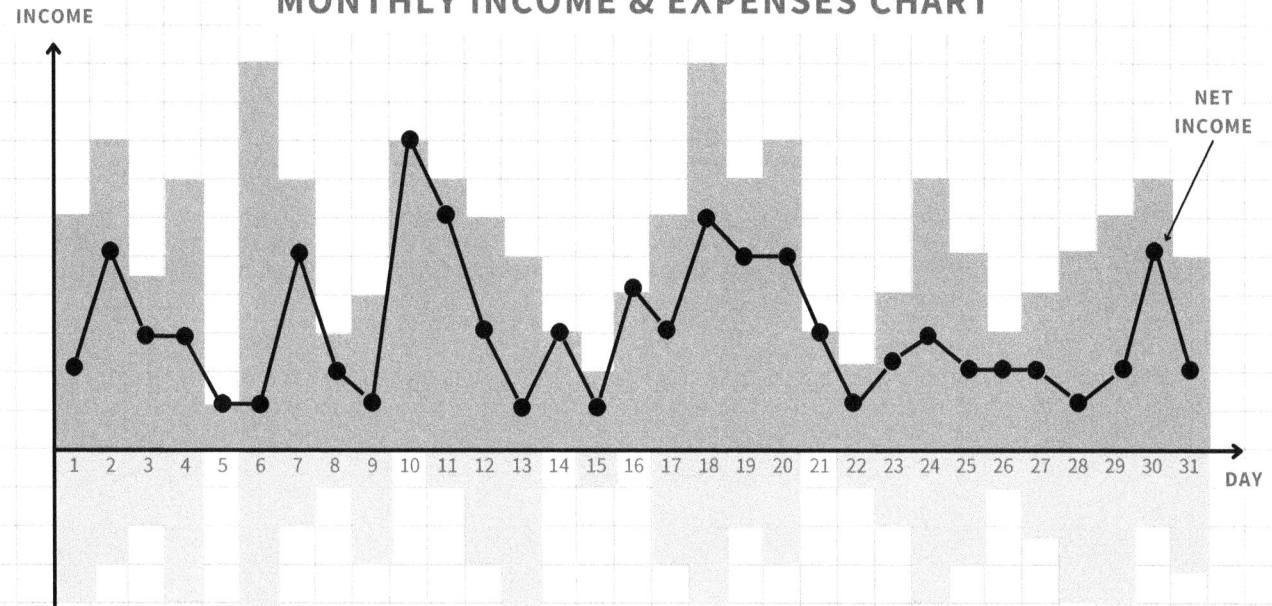

INCOME

EXPENSES

NET INCOME

DAY

1 2 3 4 5 6 7 8 9 10 11 12 13 14 15 16 17 18 19 20 21 22 23 24 25 26 27 28 29 30 31

HOW TO:

BUILD YOUR CHART USING YOUR MONTHLY INCOME & EXPENSES SUMMARY:

- CALCULATE YOUR SCALE USING THE HIGHEST NUMBER IN TERMS OF INCOME OR EXPENSES PER DAY AND DIVIDE IT BY 10 TO GET THE SIZE OF A SQUARE ON THE Y AXIS
- PLOT YOUR TOTAL DAILY INCOME AS POSITIVE BARS ON THE Y-AXIS AND YOUR TOTAL DAILY EXPENSES AS NEGATIVE BARS ON THE Y-AXIS (DIVIDE DAILY INCOME/EXPENSE BY THE SIZE OF A SQUARE TO FIND THE NUMBER OF SQUARES TO FILL)
- BUILD YOUR NET INCOME LINE CHART USING YOUR DAILY BALANCE

MONTH:

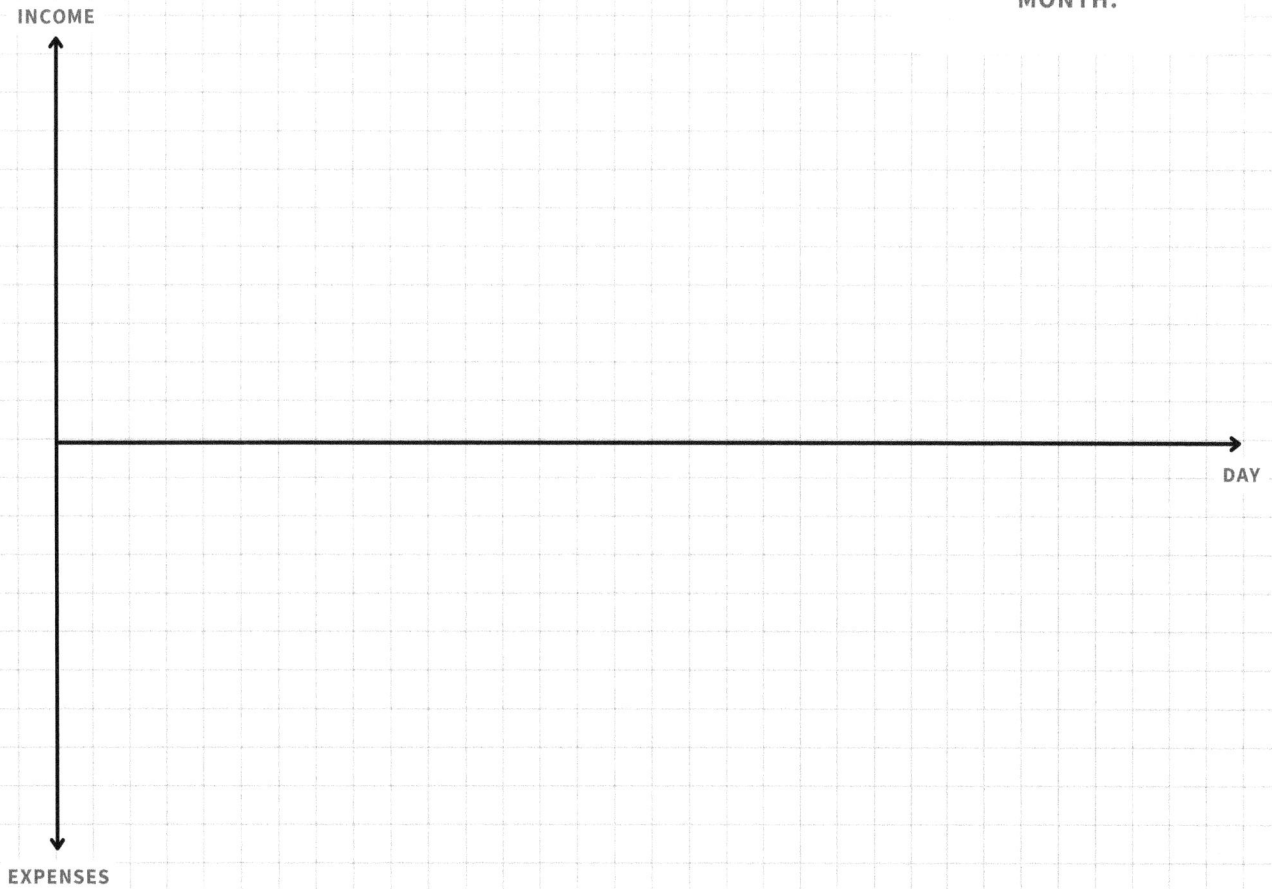

INCOME

DAY

EXPENSES

MONTHLY INCOME & EXPENSES SUMMARY

MONTH : ....

DATE	DAY	INCOME	EXPENSES	BALANCE	NOTES
1					
2					
3					
4					
5					
6					
7					
8					
9					
10					
11					
12					
13					
14					
15					
16					
17					
18					
19					
20					
21					
22					
23					
24					
25					
26					
27					
28					
29					
30					
31					
TOTAL					

MONTHLY INCOME & EXPENSES CHART

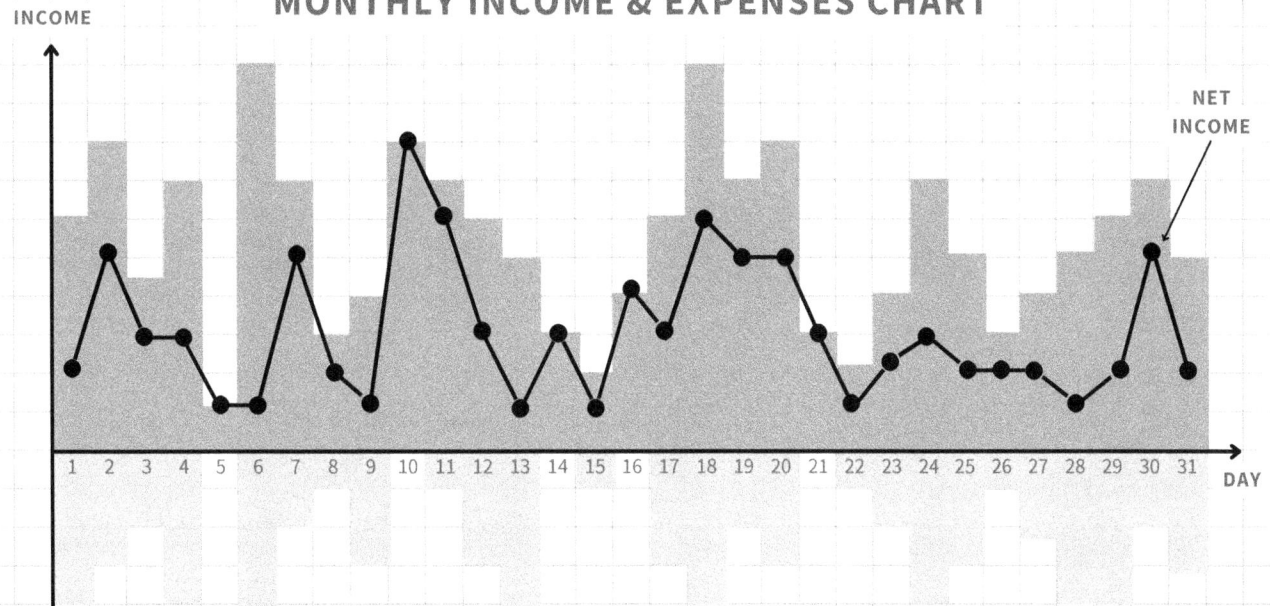

INCOME

NET INCOME

DAY

1 2 3 4 5 6 7 8 9 10 11 12 13 14 15 16 17 18 19 20 21 22 23 24 25 26 27 28 29 30 31

EXPENSES

HOW TO:

BUILD YOUR CHART USING YOUR MONTHLY INCOME & EXPENSES SUMMARY:

- CALCULATE YOUR SCALE USING THE HIGHEST NUMBER IN TERMS OF INCOME OR EXPENSES PER DAY AND DIVIDE IT BY 10 TO GET THE SIZE OF A SQUARE ON THE Y AXIS
- PLOT YOUR TOTAL DAILY INCOME AS POSITIVE BARS ON THE Y-AXIS AND YOUR TOTAL DAILY EXPENSES AS NEGATIVE BARS ON THE Y-AXIS (DIVIDE DAILY INCOME/EXPENSE BY THE SIZE OF A SQUARE TO FIND THE NUMBER OF SQUARES TO FILL)
- BUILD YOUR NET INCOME LINE CHART USING YOUR DAILY BALANCE

MONTH:

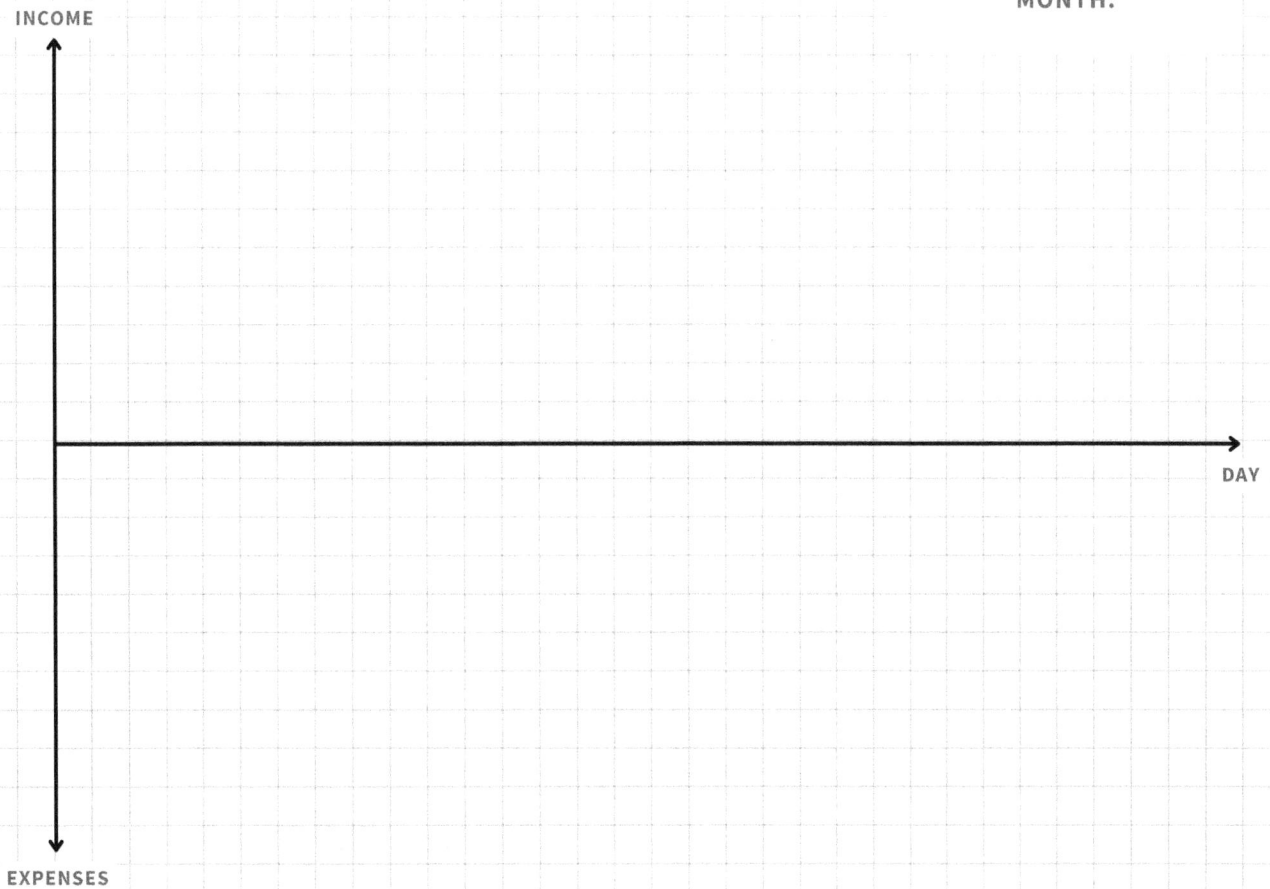

INCOME

DAY

EXPENSES

14

MONTHLY INCOME & EXPENSES SUMMARY

MONTH : ....

DATE	DAY	INCOME	EXPENSES	BALANCE	NOTES
1					
2					
3					
4					
5					
6					
7					
8					
9					
10					
11					
12					
13					
14					
15					
16					
17					
18					
19					
20					
21					
22					
23					
24					
25					
26					
27					
28					
29					
30					
31					
TOTAL					

MONTHLY INCOME & EXPENSES CHART

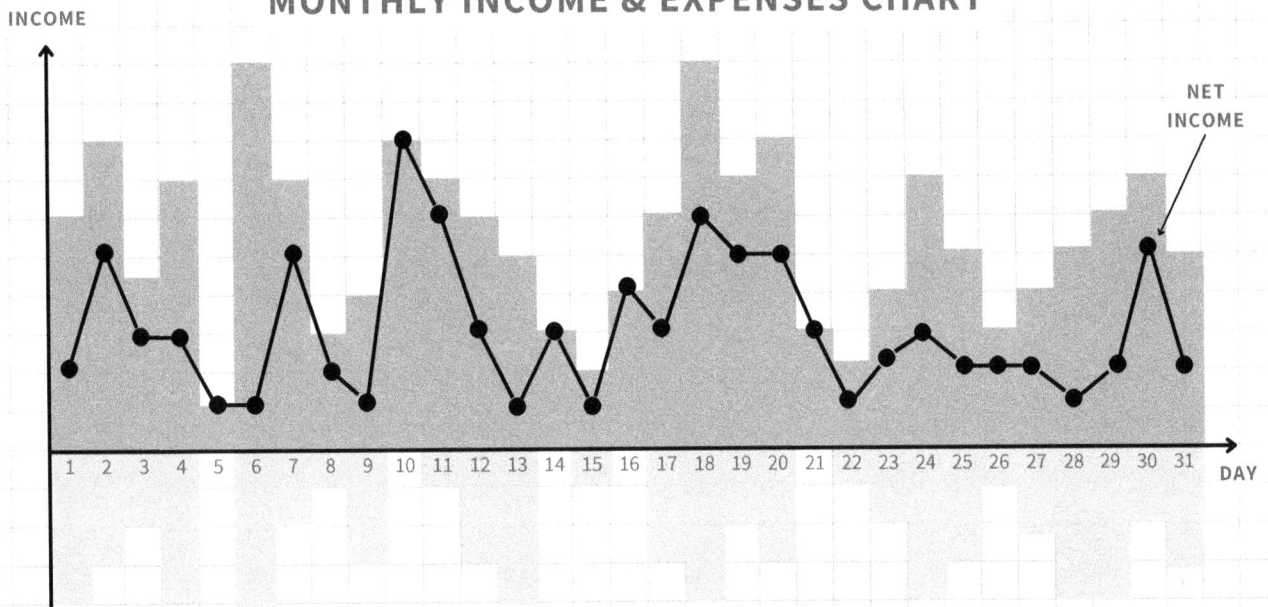

INCOME

NET INCOME

1 2 3 4 5 6 7 8 9 10 11 12 13 14 15 16 17 18 19 20 21 22 23 24 25 26 27 28 29 30 31   DAY

EXPENSES

HOW TO:

BUILD YOUR CHART USING YOUR MONTHLY INCOME & EXPENSES SUMMARY:

- CALCULATE YOUR SCALE USING THE HIGHEST NUMBER IN TERMS OF INCOME OR EXPENSES PER DAY AND DIVIDE IT BY 10 TO GET THE SIZE OF A SQUARE ON THE Y AXIS
- PLOT YOUR TOTAL DAILY INCOME AS POSITIVE BARS ON THE Y-AXIS AND YOUR TOTAL DAILY EXPENSES AS NEGATIVE BARS ON THE Y-AXIS (DIVIDE DAILY INCOME/EXPENSE BY THE SIZE OF A SQUARE TO FIND THE NUMBER OF SQUARES TO FILL)
- BUILD YOUR NET INCOME LINE CHART USING YOUR DAILY BALANCE

MONTH:

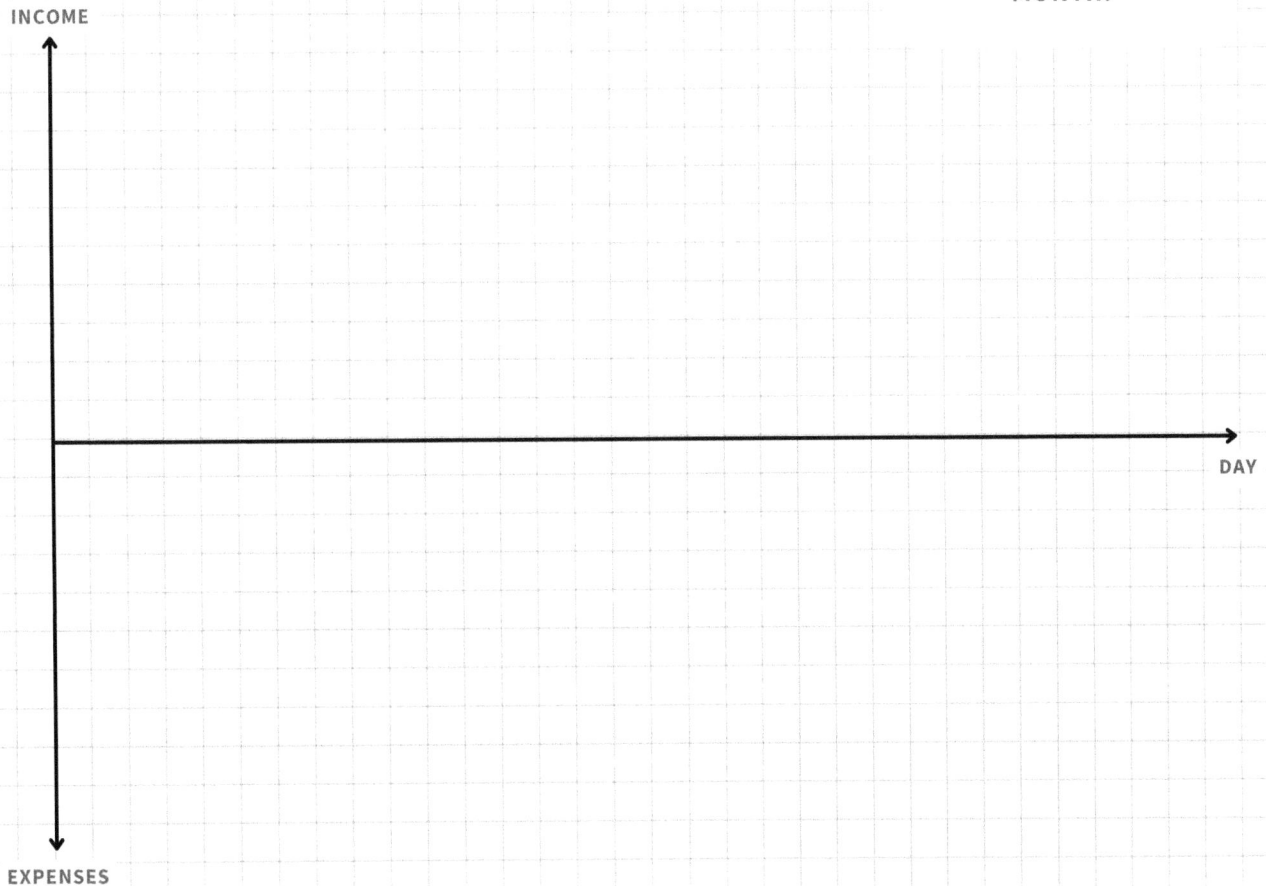

INCOME

DAY

EXPENSES

MONTHLY INCOME & EXPENSES SUMMARY

MONTH : ....

DATE	DAY	INCOME	EXPENSES	BALANCE	NOTES
1					
2					
3					
4					
5					
6					
7					
8					
9					
10					
11					
12					
13					
14					
15					
16					
17					
18					
19					
20					
21					
22					
23					
24					
25					
26					
27					
28					
29					
30					
31					
TOTAL					

MONTHLY INCOME & EXPENSES CHART

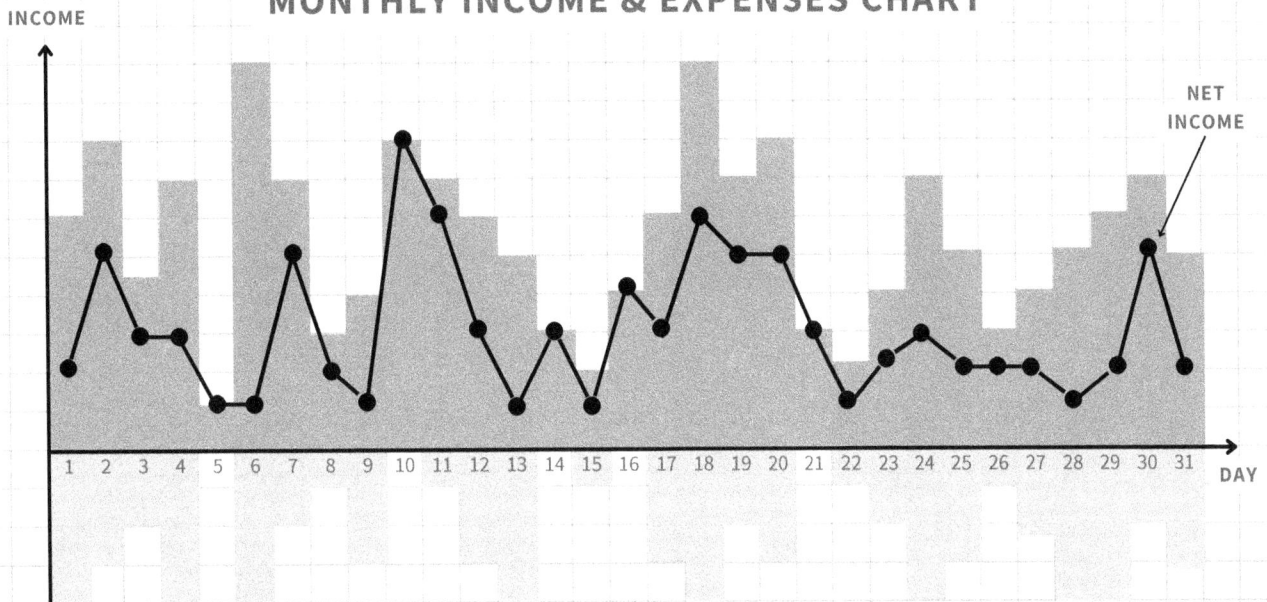

NET INCOME

HOW TO:

BUILD YOUR CHART USING YOUR MONTHLY INCOME & EXPENSES SUMMARY:
- CALCULATE YOUR SCALE USING THE HIGHEST NUMBER IN TERMS OF INCOME OR EXPENSES PER DAY AND DIVIDE IT BY 10 TO GET THE SIZE OF A SQUARE ON THE Y AXIS
- PLOT YOUR TOTAL DAILY INCOME AS POSITIVE BARS ON THE Y-AXIS AND YOUR TOTAL DAILY EXPENSES AS NEGATIVE BARS ON THE Y-AXIS (DIVIDE DAILY INCOME/EXPENSE BY THE SIZE OF A SQUARE TO FIND THE NUMBER OF SQUARES TO FILL)
- BUILD YOUR NET INCOME LINE CHART USING YOUR DAILY BALANCE

MONTH:

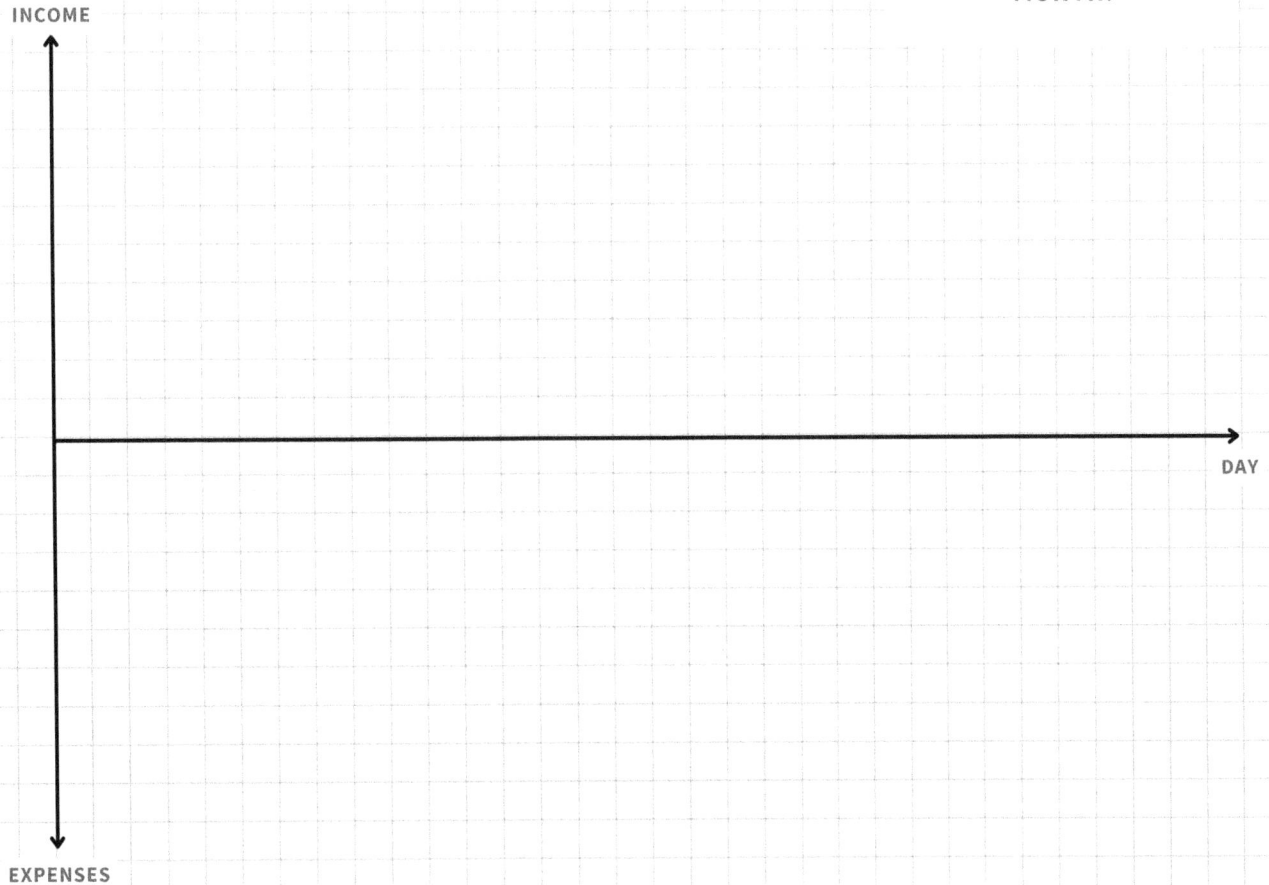

MONTHLY INCOME & EXPENSES SUMMARY

MONTH : ....

DATE	DAY	INCOME	EXPENSES	BALANCE	NOTES
1					
2					
3					
4					
5					
6					
7					
8					
9					
10					
11					
12					
13					
14					
15					
16					
17					
18					
19					
20					
21					
22					
23					
24					
25					
26					
27					
28					
29					
30					
31					
TOTAL					

MONTHLY INCOME & EXPENSES CHART

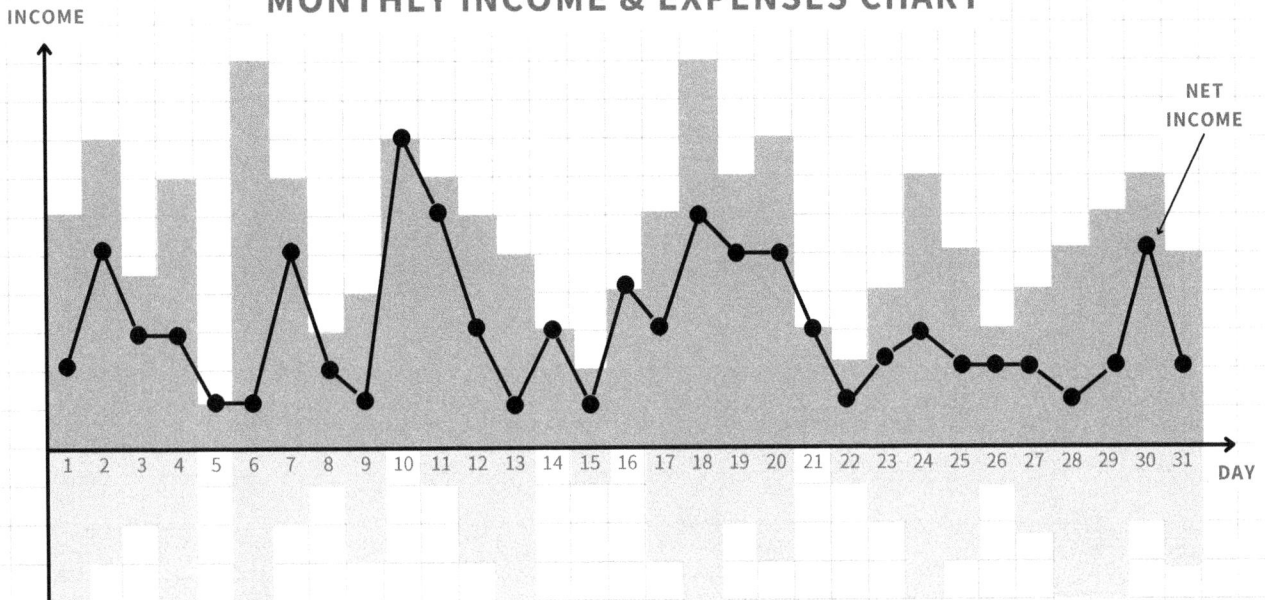

HOW TO:

BUILD YOUR CHART USING YOUR MONTHLY INCOME & EXPENSES SUMMARY:

- CALCULATE YOUR SCALE USING THE HIGHEST NUMBER IN TERMS OF INCOME OR EXPENSES PER DAY AND DIVIDE IT BY 10 TO GET THE SIZE OF A SQUARE ON THE Y AXIS
- PLOT YOUR TOTAL DAILY INCOME AS POSITIVE BARS ON THE Y-AXIS AND YOUR TOTAL DAILY EXPENSES AS NEGATIVE BARS ON THE Y-AXIS (DIVIDE DAILY INCOME/EXPENSE BY THE SIZE OF A SQUARE TO FIND THE NUMBER OF SQUARES TO FILL)
- BUILD YOUR NET INCOME LINE CHART USING YOUR DAILY BALANCE

MONTH:

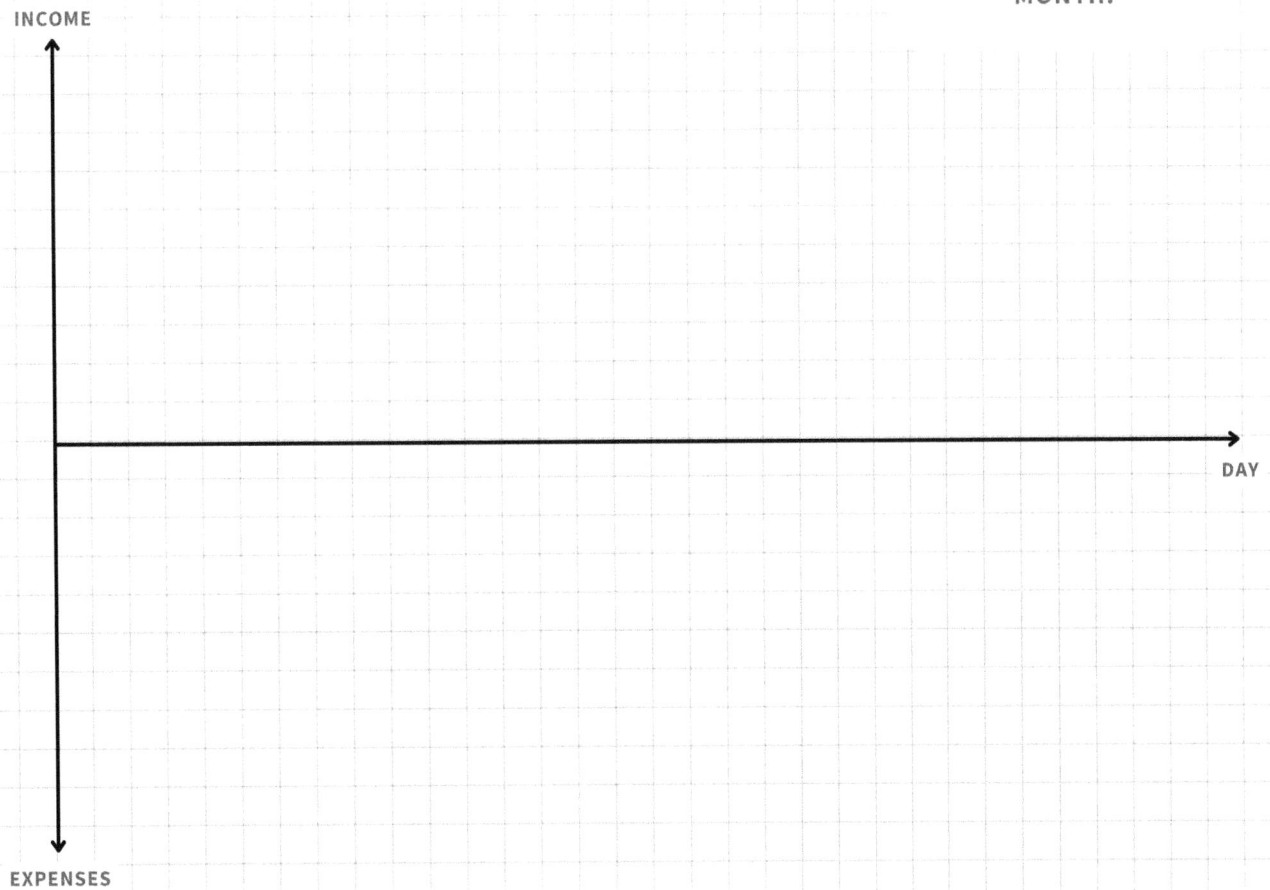

20

MONTHLY INCOME & EXPENSES SUMMARY

MONTH : ....

DATE	DAY	INCOME	EXPENSES	BALANCE	NOTES
1					
2					
3					
4					
5					
6					
7					
8					
9					
10					
11					
12					
13					
14					
15					
16					
17					
18					
19					
20					
21					
22					
23					
24					
25					
26					
27					
28					
29					
30					
31					
TOTAL					

MONTHLY INCOME & EXPENSES CHART

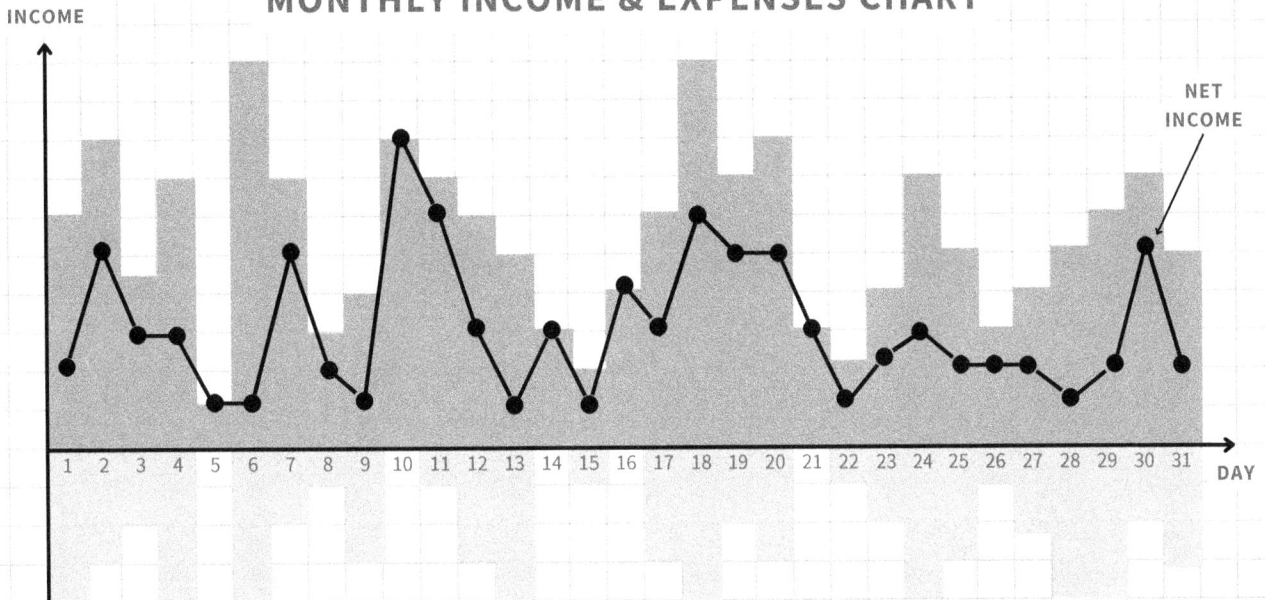

HOW TO:

BUILD YOUR CHART USING YOUR MONTHLY INCOME & EXPENSES SUMMARY:

- CALCULATE YOUR SCALE USING THE HIGHEST NUMBER IN TERMS OF INCOME OR EXPENSES PER DAY AND DIVIDE IT BY 10 TO GET THE SIZE OF A SQUARE ON THE Y AXIS
- PLOT YOUR TOTAL DAILY INCOME AS POSITIVE BARS ON THE Y-AXIS AND YOUR TOTAL DAILY EXPENSES AS NEGATIVE BARS ON THE Y-AXIS (DIVIDE DAILY INCOME/EXPENSE BY THE SIZE OF A SQUARE TO FIND THE NUMBER OF SQUARES TO FILL)
- BUILD YOUR NET INCOME LINE CHART USING YOUR DAILY BALANCE

MONTH:

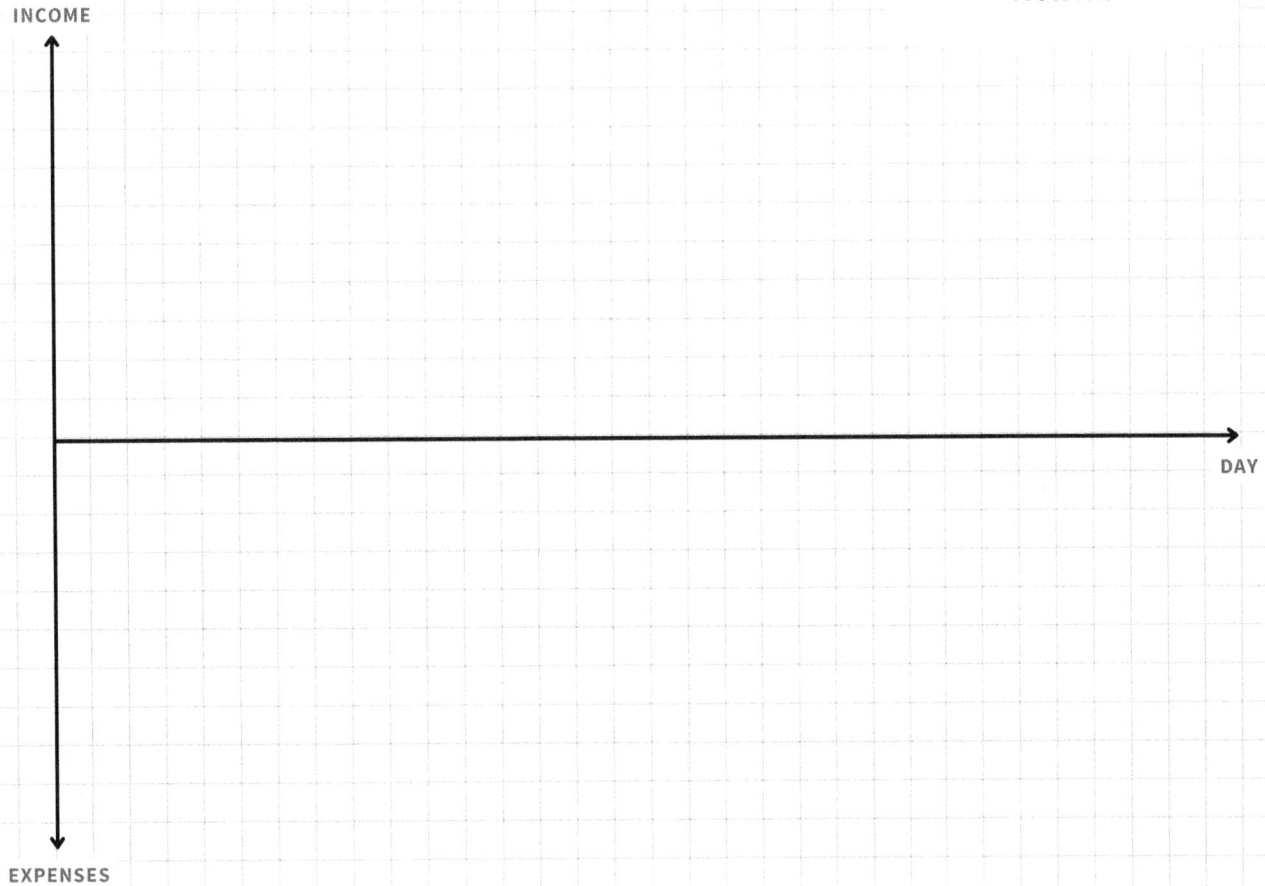

22

MONTHLY INCOME & EXPENSES SUMMARY

MONTH : ....

DATE	DAY	INCOME	EXPENSES	BALANCE	NOTES
1					
2					
3					
4					
5					
6					
7					
8					
9					
10					
11					
12					
13					
14					
15					
16					
17					
18					
19					
20					
21					
22					
23					
24					
25					
26					
27					
28					
29					
30					
31					
TOTAL					

MONTHLY INCOME & EXPENSES CHART

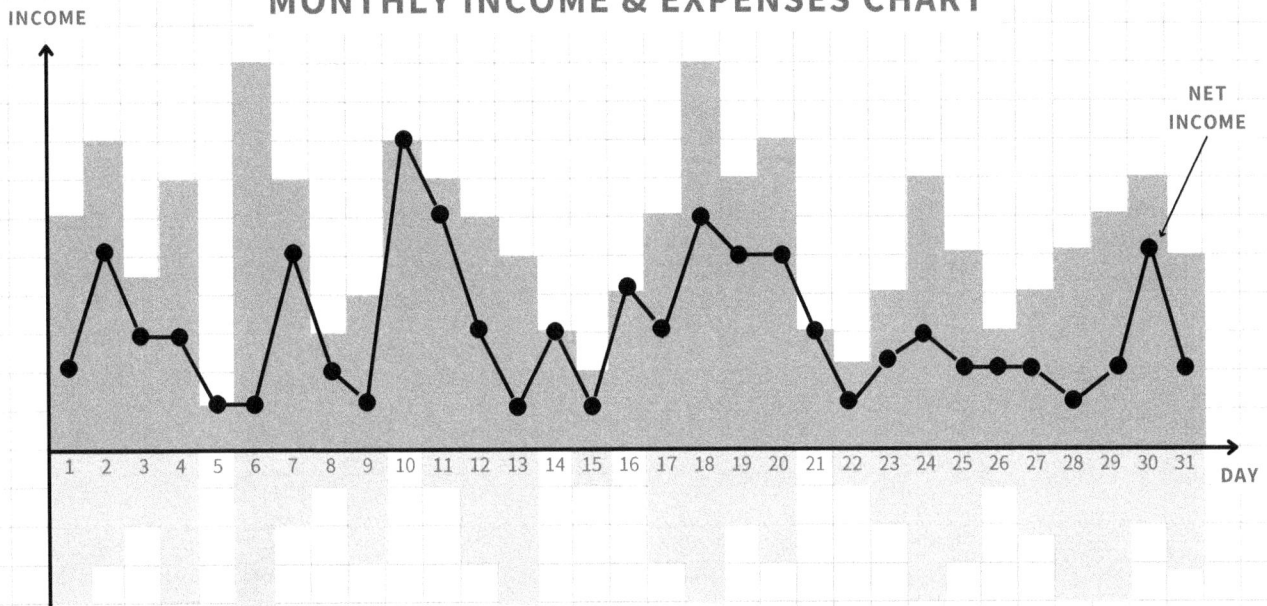

INCOME

NET INCOME

1 2 3 4 5 6 7 8 9 10 11 12 13 14 15 16 17 18 19 20 21 22 23 24 25 26 27 28 29 30 31 **DAY**

EXPENSES

HOW TO:

BUILD YOUR CHART USING YOUR MONTHLY INCOME & EXPENSES SUMMARY:

- CALCULATE YOUR SCALE USING THE HIGHEST NUMBER IN TERMS OF INCOME OR EXPENSES PER DAY AND DIVIDE IT BY 10 TO GET THE SIZE OF A SQUARE ON THE Y AXIS
- PLOT YOUR TOTAL DAILY INCOME AS POSITIVE BARS ON THE Y-AXIS AND YOUR TOTAL DAILY EXPENSES AS NEGATIVE BARS ON THE Y-AXIS (DIVIDE DAILY INCOME/EXPENSE BY THE SIZE OF A SQUARE TO FIND THE NUMBER OF SQUARES TO FILL)
- BUILD YOUR NET INCOME LINE CHART USING YOUR DAILY BALANCE

MONTH:

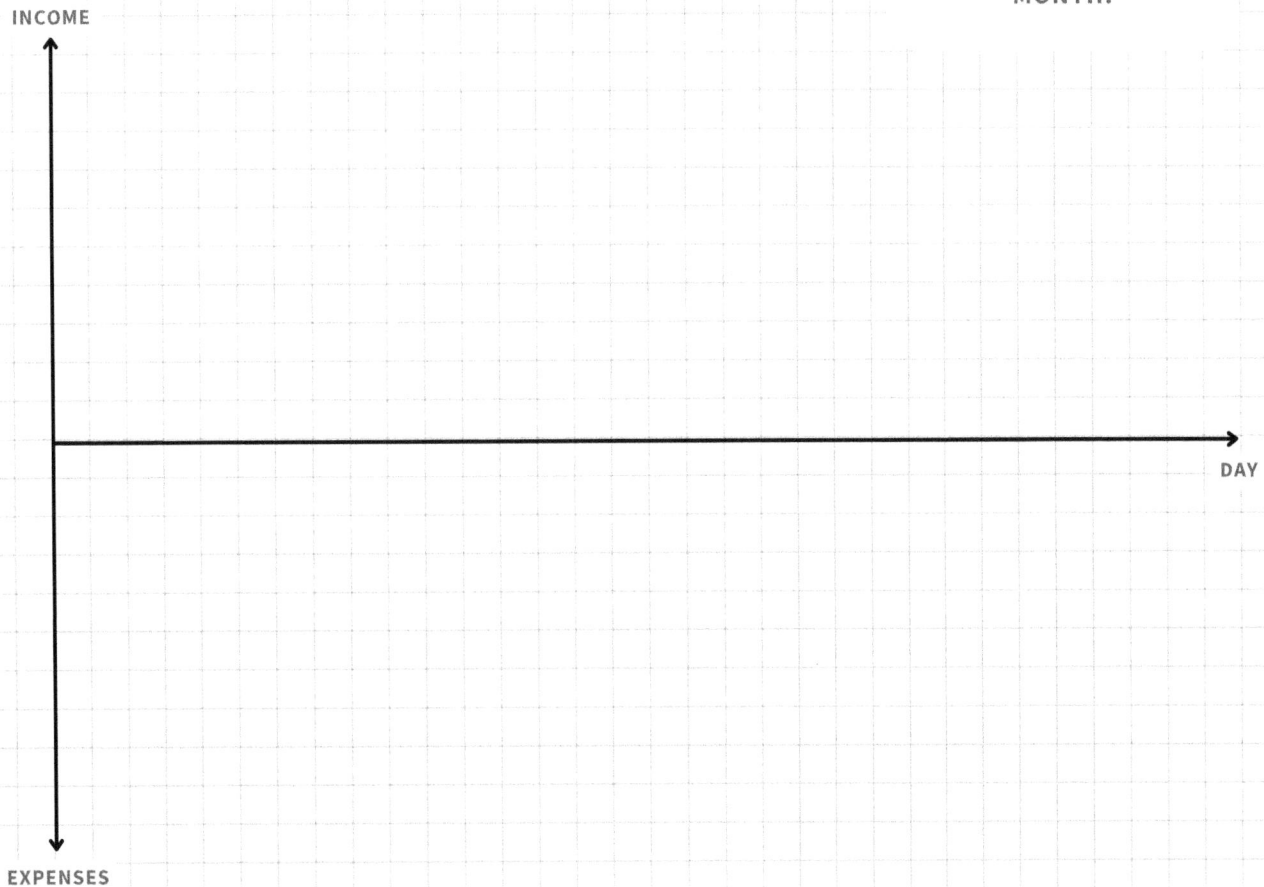

INCOME

DAY

EXPENSES

MONTHLY INCOME & EXPENSES SUMMARY

MONTH : ....

DATE	DAY	INCOME	EXPENSES	BALANCE	NOTES
1					
2					
3					
4					
5					
6					
7					
8					
9					
10					
11					
12					
13					
14					
15					
16					
17					
18					
19					
20					
21					
22					
23					
24					
25					
26					
27					
28					
29					
30					
31					
TOTAL					

MONTHLY INCOME & EXPENSES CHART

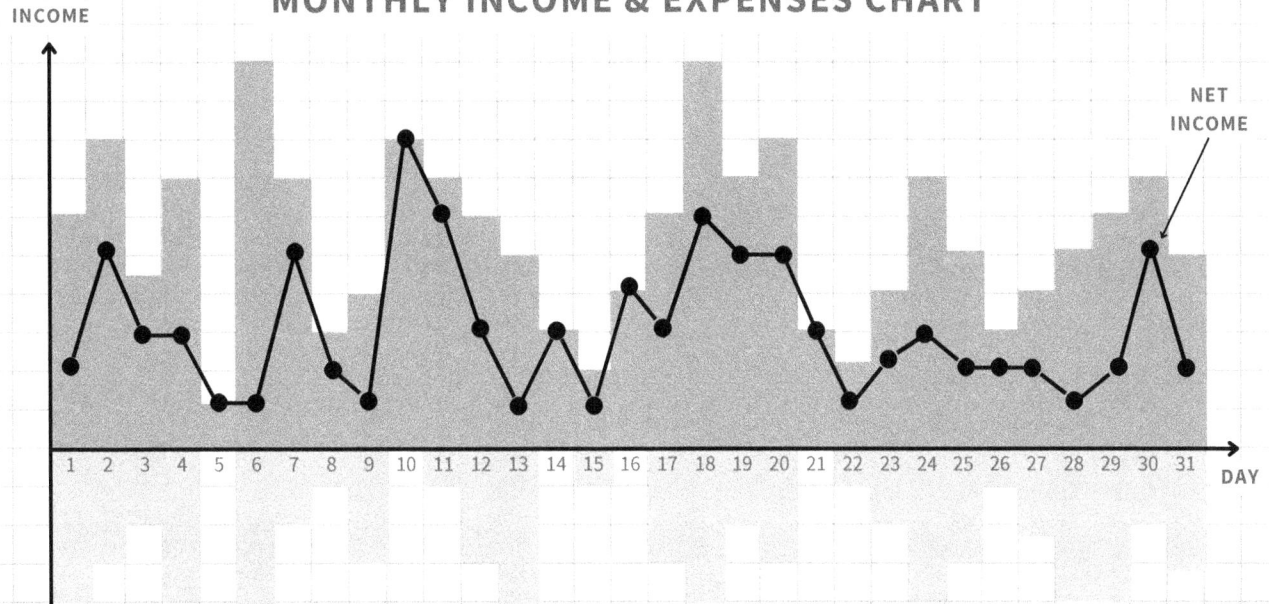

INCOME

NET INCOME

DAY

1 2 3 4 5 6 7 8 9 10 11 12 13 14 15 16 17 18 19 20 21 22 23 24 25 26 27 28 29 30 31

EXPENSES

HOW TO:

BUILD YOUR CHART USING YOUR MONTHLY INCOME & EXPENSES SUMMARY:

- CALCULATE YOUR SCALE USING THE HIGHEST NUMBER IN TERMS OF INCOME OR EXPENSES PER DAY AND DIVIDE IT BY 10 TO GET THE SIZE OF A SQUARE ON THE Y AXIS
- PLOT YOUR TOTAL DAILY INCOME AS POSITIVE BARS ON THE Y-AXIS AND YOUR TOTAL DAILY EXPENSES AS NEGATIVE BARS ON THE Y-AXIS (DIVIDE DAILY INCOME/EXPENSE BY THE SIZE OF A SQUARE TO FIND THE NUMBER OF SQUARES TO FILL)
- BUILD YOUR NET INCOME LINE CHART USING YOUR DAILY BALANCE

MONTH:

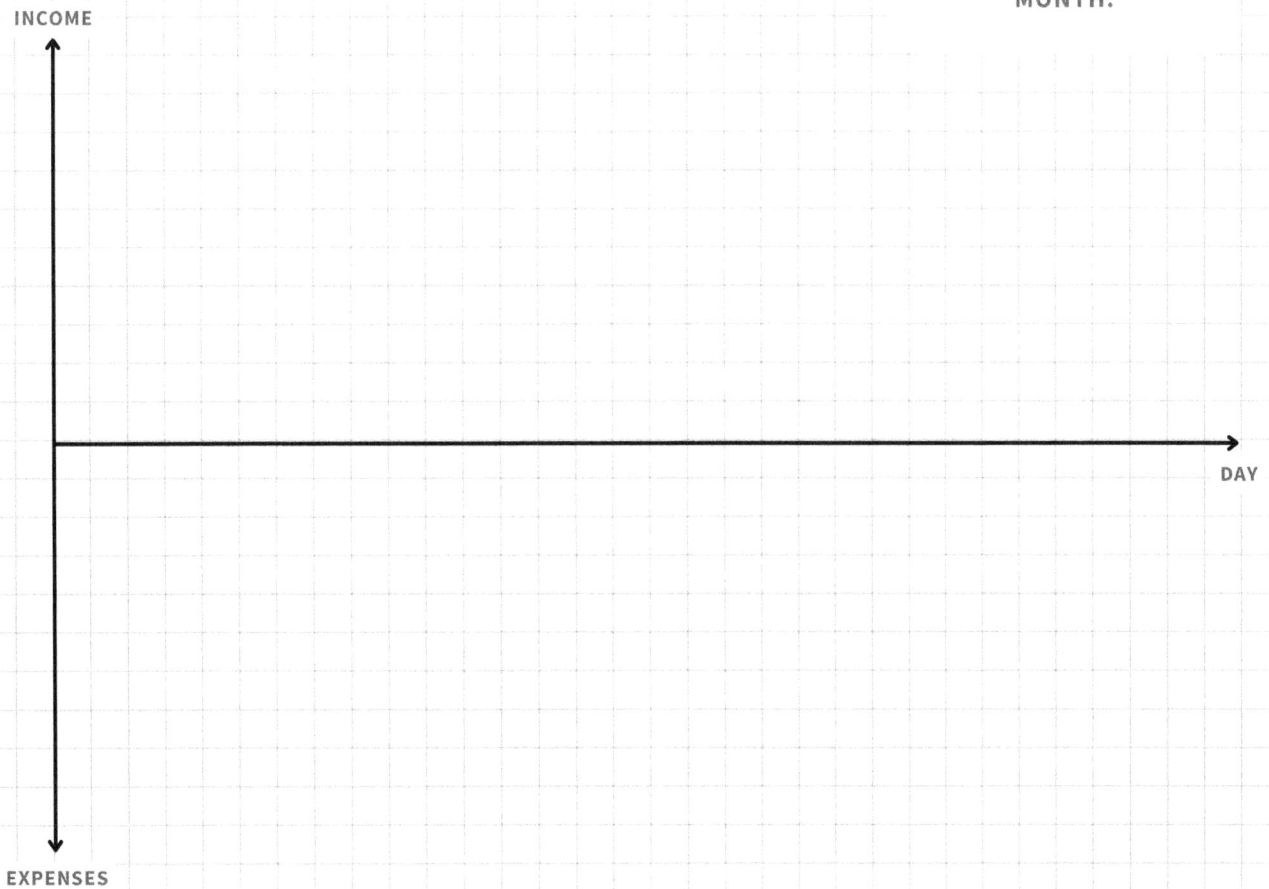

INCOME

DAY

EXPENSES

DAILY INCOME & EXPENSES

MONTH : ....

NO	DATE	DETAILS	INCOME	EXPENSES	MODE OF PAYMENT	BALANCE

DAILY INCOME & EXPENSES

MONTH : ....

NO	DATE	DETAILS	INCOME	EXPENSES	MODE OF PAYMENT	BALANCE

DAILY INCOME & EXPENSES

MONTH : ....

NO	DATE	DETAILS	INCOME	EXPENSES	MODE OF PAYMENT	BALANCE

DAILY INCOME & EXPENSES

MONTH : _____

NO	DATE	DETAILS	INCOME	EXPENSES	MODE OF PAYMENT	BALANCE

DAILY INCOME & EXPENSES

MONTH : ....

NO	DATE	DETAILS	INCOME	EXPENSES	MODE OF PAYMENT	BALANCE

DAILY INCOME & EXPENSES

MONTH : ....

NO	DATE	DETAILS	INCOME	EXPENSES	MODE OF PAYMENT	BALANCE

DAILY INCOME & EXPENSES

MONTH : ....

NO	DATE	DETAILS	INCOME	EXPENSES	MODE OF PAYMENT	BALANCE

DAILY INCOME & EXPENSES

MONTH : ....

NO	DATE	DETAILS	INCOME	EXPENSES	MODE OF PAYMENT	BALANCE

DAILY INCOME & EXPENSES

MONTH : ....

NO	DATE	DETAILS	INCOME	EXPENSES	MODE OF PAYMENT	BALANCE

DAILY INCOME & EXPENSES

MONTH : ....

NO	DATE	DETAILS	INCOME	EXPENSES	MODE OF PAYMENT	BALANCE

DAILY INCOME & EXPENSES

MONTH : _____

NO	DATE	DETAILS	INCOME	EXPENSES	MODE OF PAYMENT	BALANCE

DAILY INCOME & EXPENSES

MONTH : ....

NO	DATE	DETAILS	INCOME	EXPENSES	MODE OF PAYMENT	BALANCE

DAILY INCOME & EXPENSES

MONTH : ....

NO	DATE	DETAILS	INCOME	EXPENSES	MODE OF PAYMENT	BALANCE

DAILY INCOME & EXPENSES

MONTH : ....

NO	DATE	DETAILS	INCOME	EXPENSES	MODE OF PAYMENT	BALANCE

DAILY INCOME & EXPENSES

MONTH : ....

NO	DATE	DETAILS	INCOME	EXPENSES	MODE OF PAYMENT	BALANCE

DAILY INCOME & EXPENSES

MONTH : ....

NO	DATE	DETAILS	INCOME		EXPENSES		MODE OF PAYMENT	BALANCE	

DAILY INCOME & EXPENSES

MONTH : ....

NO	DATE	DETAILS	INCOME	EXPENSES	MODE OF PAYMENT	BALANCE

DAILY INCOME & EXPENSES

MONTH : ....

NO	DATE	DETAILS	INCOME	EXPENSES	MODE OF PAYMENT	BALANCE

DAILY INCOME & EXPENSES

MONTH : ....

NO	DATE	DETAILS	INCOME		EXPENSES		MODE OF PAYMENT	BALANCE	

DAILY INCOME & EXPENSES

MONTH : ....

NO	DATE	DETAILS	INCOME	EXPENSES	MODE OF PAYMENT	BALANCE

DAILY INCOME & EXPENSES

MONTH : ....

NO	DATE	DETAILS	INCOME	EXPENSES	MODE OF PAYMENT	BALANCE

DAILY INCOME & EXPENSES

MONTH : ....

NO	DATE	DETAILS	INCOME	EXPENSES	MODE OF PAYMENT	BALANCE

DAILY INCOME & EXPENSES

MONTH : ....

NO	DATE	DETAILS	INCOME	EXPENSES	MODE OF PAYMENT	BALANCE

DAILY INCOME & EXPENSES

MONTH : ....

NO	DATE	DETAILS	INCOME	EXPENSES	MODE OF PAYMENT	BALANCE

DAILY INCOME & EXPENSES

MONTH : ....

NO	DATE	DETAILS	INCOME	EXPENSES	MODE OF PAYMENT	BALANCE

DAILY INCOME & EXPENSES

MONTH : ....

NO	DATE	DETAILS	INCOME	EXPENSES	MODE OF PAYMENT	BALANCE

DAILY INCOME & EXPENSES

MONTH : ....

NO	DATE	DETAILS	INCOME	EXPENSES	MODE OF PAYMENT	BALANCE

DAILY INCOME & EXPENSES

MONTH : ....

NO	DATE	DETAILS	INCOME	EXPENSES	MODE OF PAYMENT	BALANCE

DAILY INCOME & EXPENSES

MONTH : ....

NO	DATE	DETAILS	INCOME	EXPENSES	MODE OF PAYMENT	BALANCE

DAILY INCOME & EXPENSES

MONTH : _____

NO	DATE	DETAILS	INCOME	EXPENSES	MODE OF PAYMENT	BALANCE

DAILY INCOME & EXPENSES

MONTH : ....

NO	DATE	DETAILS	INCOME	EXPENSES	MODE OF PAYMENT	BALANCE

DAILY INCOME & EXPENSES

MONTH : ....

NO	DATE	DETAILS	INCOME	EXPENSES	MODE OF PAYMENT	BALANCE

DAILY INCOME & EXPENSES

MONTH : ....

NO	DATE	DETAILS	INCOME	EXPENSES	MODE OF PAYMENT	BALANCE

DAILY INCOME & EXPENSES

MONTH : ....

NO	DATE	DETAILS	INCOME	EXPENSES	MODE OF PAYMENT	BALANCE

DAILY INCOME & EXPENSES

MONTH : _____

NO	DATE	DETAILS	INCOME	EXPENSES	MODE OF PAYMENT	BALANCE

DAILY INCOME & EXPENSES

MONTH : ....

NO	DATE	DETAILS	INCOME	EXPENSES	MODE OF PAYMENT	BALANCE

DAILY INCOME & EXPENSES

MONTH : ....

NO	DATE	DETAILS	INCOME	EXPENSES	MODE OF PAYMENT	BALANCE

DAILY INCOME & EXPENSES

MONTH : ....

NO	DATE	DETAILS	INCOME	EXPENSES	MODE OF PAYMENT	BALANCE

DAILY INCOME & EXPENSES

MONTH : ....

NO	DATE	DETAILS	INCOME	EXPENSES	MODE OF PAYMENT	BALANCE

DAILY INCOME & EXPENSES

MONTH : ....

NO	DATE	DETAILS	INCOME	EXPENSES	MODE OF PAYMENT	BALANCE

DAILY INCOME & EXPENSES

MONTH : ....

NO	DATE	DETAILS	INCOME	EXPENSES	MODE OF PAYMENT	BALANCE

DAILY INCOME & EXPENSES

MONTH : ....

NO	DATE	DETAILS	INCOME	EXPENSES	MODE OF PAYMENT	BALANCE

DAILY INCOME & EXPENSES

MONTH : ....

NO	DATE	DETAILS	INCOME	EXPENSES	MODE OF PAYMENT	BALANCE

DAILY INCOME & EXPENSES

MONTH : ....

NO	DATE	DETAILS	INCOME	EXPENSES	MODE OF PAYMENT	BALANCE

DAILY INCOME & EXPENSES

MONTH : ....

NO	DATE	DETAILS	INCOME	EXPENSES	MODE OF PAYMENT	BALANCE

DAILY INCOME & EXPENSES

MONTH : ....

NO	DATE	DETAILS	INCOME	EXPENSES	MODE OF PAYMENT	BALANCE

DAILY INCOME & EXPENSES

MONTH : ....

NO	DATE	DETAILS	INCOME	EXPENSES	MODE OF PAYMENT	BALANCE

DAILY INCOME & EXPENSES

MONTH : ....

NO	DATE	DETAILS	INCOME	EXPENSES	MODE OF PAYMENT	BALANCE

DAILY INCOME & EXPENSES

MONTH : ....

NO	DATE	DETAILS	INCOME	EXPENSES	MODE OF PAYMENT	BALANCE

DAILY INCOME & EXPENSES

MONTH : _____

NO	DATE	DETAILS	INCOME	EXPENSES	MODE OF PAYMENT	BALANCE

DAILY INCOME & EXPENSES

MONTH : ....

NO	DATE	DETAILS	INCOME	EXPENSES	MODE OF PAYMENT	BALANCE

DAILY INCOME & EXPENSES

MONTH : ....

NO	DATE	DETAILS	INCOME	EXPENSES	MODE OF PAYMENT	BALANCE

DAILY INCOME & EXPENSES

MONTH : _____

NO	DATE	DETAILS	INCOME	EXPENSES	MODE OF PAYMENT	BALANCE

DAILY INCOME & EXPENSES

MONTH : ....

NO	DATE	DETAILS	INCOME	EXPENSES	MODE OF PAYMENT	BALANCE

DAILY INCOME & EXPENSES

MONTH : ....

NO	DATE	DETAILS	INCOME	EXPENSES	MODE OF PAYMENT	BALANCE

DAILY INCOME & EXPENSES

MONTH : ....

NO	DATE	DETAILS	INCOME	EXPENSES	MODE OF PAYMENT	BALANCE

DAILY INCOME & EXPENSES

MONTH : ....

NO	DATE	DETAILS	INCOME	EXPENSES	MODE OF PAYMENT	BALANCE

DAILY INCOME & EXPENSES

MONTH : ....

NO	DATE	DETAILS	INCOME	EXPENSES	MODE OF PAYMENT	BALANCE

DAILY INCOME & EXPENSES

MONTH : ....

NO	DATE	DETAILS	INCOME	EXPENSES	MODE OF PAYMENT	BALANCE

DAILY INCOME & EXPENSES

MONTH : ....

NO	DATE	DETAILS	INCOME	EXPENSES	MODE OF PAYMENT	BALANCE

DAILY INCOME & EXPENSES

MONTH : ....

NO	DATE	DETAILS	INCOME	EXPENSES	MODE OF PAYMENT	BALANCE

DAILY INCOME & EXPENSES

MONTH : ....

NO	DATE	DETAILS	INCOME	EXPENSES	MODE OF PAYMENT	BALANCE

DAILY INCOME & EXPENSES

MONTH : _____

NO	DATE	DETAILS	INCOME	EXPENSES	MODE OF PAYMENT	BALANCE

DAILY INCOME & EXPENSES

MONTH : ....

NO	DATE	DETAILS	INCOME	EXPENSES	MODE OF PAYMENT	BALANCE

DAILY INCOME & EXPENSES

MONTH : ....

NO	DATE	DETAILS	INCOME	EXPENSES	MODE OF PAYMENT	BALANCE

DAILY INCOME & EXPENSES

MONTH : _____

NO	DATE	DETAILS	INCOME	EXPENSES	MODE OF PAYMENT	BALANCE

DAILY INCOME & EXPENSES

MONTH : ....

NO	DATE	DETAILS	INCOME	EXPENSES	MODE OF PAYMENT	BALANCE

DAILY INCOME & EXPENSES

MONTH : ....

NO	DATE	DETAILS	INCOME	EXPENSES	MODE OF PAYMENT	BALANCE

DAILY INCOME & EXPENSES

MONTH : ....

NO	DATE	DETAILS	INCOME	EXPENSES	MODE OF PAYMENT	BALANCE

DAILY INCOME & EXPENSES

MONTH : ....

NO	DATE	DETAILS	INCOME	EXPENSES	MODE OF PAYMENT	BALANCE

DAILY INCOME & EXPENSES

MONTH : _____

NO	DATE	DETAILS	INCOME	EXPENSES	MODE OF PAYMENT	BALANCE

DAILY INCOME & EXPENSES

MONTH : ....

NO	DATE	DETAILS	INCOME	EXPENSES	MODE OF PAYMENT	BALANCE

DAILY INCOME & EXPENSES

MONTH : ....

NO	DATE	DETAILS	INCOME	EXPENSES	MODE OF PAYMENT	BALANCE

DAILY INCOME & EXPENSES

MONTH : ....

NO	DATE	DETAILS	INCOME	EXPENSES	MODE OF PAYMENT	BALANCE

DAILY INCOME & EXPENSES

MONTH : ....

NO	DATE	DETAILS	INCOME	EXPENSES	MODE OF PAYMENT	BALANCE

DAILY INCOME & EXPENSES

MONTH : ....

NO	DATE	DETAILS	INCOME	EXPENSES	MODE OF PAYMENT	BALANCE

DAILY INCOME & EXPENSES

MONTH : ....

NO	DATE	DETAILS	INCOME	EXPENSES	MODE OF PAYMENT	BALANCE

DAILY INCOME & EXPENSES

MONTH : ....

NO	DATE	DETAILS	INCOME	EXPENSES	MODE OF PAYMENT	BALANCE

DAILY INCOME & EXPENSES

MONTH : ....

NO	DATE	DETAILS	INCOME	EXPENSES	MODE OF PAYMENT	BALANCE

DAILY INCOME & EXPENSES

MONTH : ....

NO	DATE	DETAILS	INCOME	EXPENSES	MODE OF PAYMENT	BALANCE

DAILY INCOME & EXPENSES

MONTH : ....

NO	DATE	DETAILS	INCOME	EXPENSES	MODE OF PAYMENT	BALANCE

DAILY INCOME & EXPENSES

MONTH : _____

NO	DATE	DETAILS	INCOME	EXPENSES	MODE OF PAYMENT	BALANCE

DAILY INCOME & EXPENSES

MONTH : ....

NO	DATE	DETAILS	INCOME	EXPENSES	MODE OF PAYMENT	BALANCE

DAILY INCOME & EXPENSES

MONTH : _____

NO	DATE	DETAILS	INCOME	EXPENSES	MODE OF PAYMENT	BALANCE

DAILY INCOME & EXPENSES

MONTH : ....

NO	DATE	DETAILS	INCOME	EXPENSES	MODE OF PAYMENT	BALANCE

DAILY INCOME & EXPENSES

MONTH : ....

NO	DATE	DETAILS	INCOME	EXPENSES	MODE OF PAYMENT	BALANCE

DAILY INCOME & EXPENSES

MONTH : ....

NO	DATE	DETAILS	INCOME	EXPENSES	MODE OF PAYMENT	BALANCE

DAILY INCOME & EXPENSES

MONTH : _____

NO	DATE	DETAILS	INCOME	EXPENSES	MODE OF PAYMENT	BALANCE

DAILY INCOME & EXPENSES

MONTH : ....

NO	DATE	DETAILS	INCOME		EXPENSES		MODE OF PAYMENT	BALANCE	

DAILY INCOME & EXPENSES

MONTH : _____

NO	DATE	DETAILS	INCOME	EXPENSES	MODE OF PAYMENT	BALANCE

www.ingramcontent.com/pod-product-compliance
Lightning Source LLC
Chambersburg PA
CBHW051757200326
41597CB00025B/4594

* 9 7 8 1 8 0 3 9 3 2 1 8 7 *